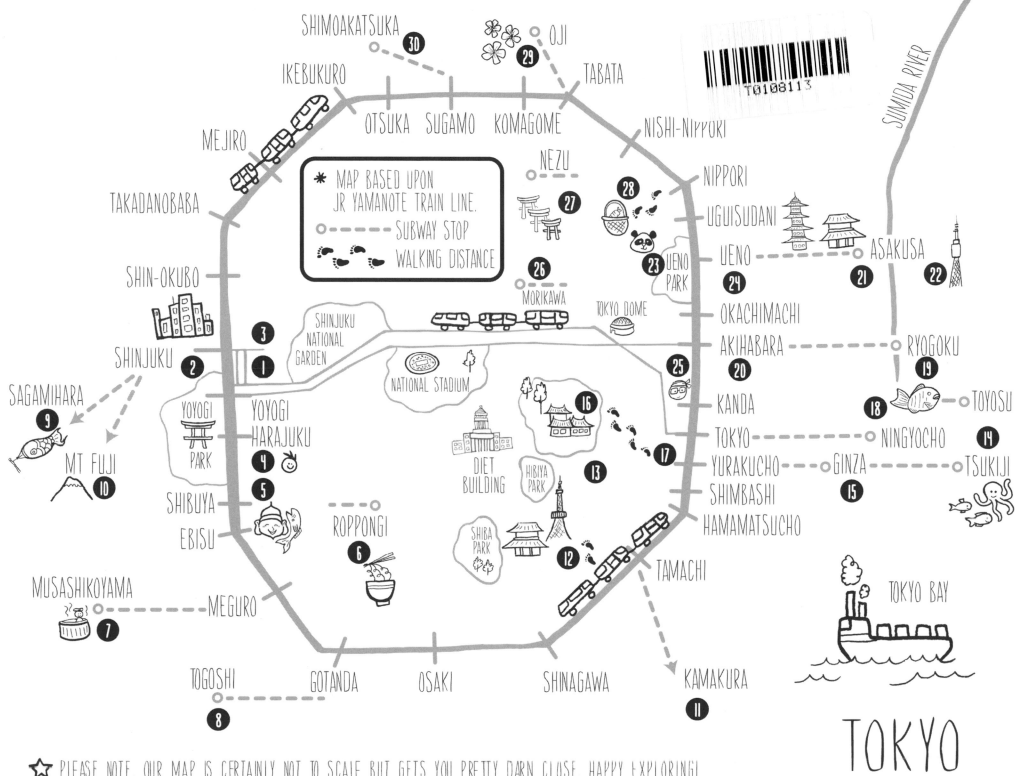

TOKYO

SUMIDA RIVER

* MAP BASED UPON
JR YAMANOTE TRAIN LINE.

○ - - - SUBWAY STOP

👣👣 WALKING DISTANCE

SHIMOAKATSUKA ③⓪
OJI ②⑨
TABATA
IKEBUKURO
MEJIRO
OTSUKA SUGAMO KOMAGOME
NISHI-NIPPORI
TAKADANOBABA
NEZU
NIPPORI
②⑧
②⑦ UGUISUDANI
SHIN-OKUBO
②⑥ ②③ UENO PARK
UENO ASAKUSA ②②
MORIKAWA ②④ ②①
SHINJUKU NATIONAL GARDEN
③ OKACHIMACHI
TOKYO DOME
② ①
NATIONAL STADIUM
AKIHABARA RYOGOKU ①⑨
SAGAMIHARA
②⑤
KANDA
⑨
YOYOGI HARAJUKU
②⓪
MT FUJI ⑩
④
①⑧ TOYOSU
YOYOGI PARK
①⑥ TOKYO NINGYOCHO ①④
SHIBUYA
DIET BUILDING
⑤
HIBIYA PARK
①③ ①⑦ YURAKUCHO GINZA TSUKIJI
EBISU
ROPPONGI
⑥ ①⑤
SHIMBASHI
SHIBA PARK
HAMAMATSUCHO
MUSASHIKOYAMA
MEGURO
①②
⑦ TAMACHI
TOKYO BAY
TOGOSHI GOTANDA OSAKI SHINAGAWA KAMAKURA
⑧ ①①

☆ PLEASE NOTE, OUR MAP IS CERTAINLY NOT TO SCALE BUT GETS YOU PRETTY DARN CLOSE. HAPPY EXPLORING!

T0108113

COLORFUL TOKYO LOCATIONS

Please note all the information was correct at the time of publication, but as with all things in life it is subject to change. Happy exploring!

Shinjuku 新宿   Words cannot describe the stunning array of colorful neon that advertises the Shinjuku district's many entertainment, business and shopping establishments. The abundance of sights and sounds in this district exemplify modern Tokyo. If you visit Tokyo, you're bound to cross through Shinjuku as its train station is the world's busiest. Make a stop and explore!

Tokyo View 東京の景色   An excellent way to appreciate the vast size of Tokyo is to take in the view from the observation decks on the 45th floor of the Tokyo Metropolitan Government Buildings. Stunning views can be seen from all sides and entry is free. www.tokyometro.jp/en/attractions/metropolitan_govt_bldg/

Omoide Yokocho 思い出横丁   Old meets new along the underpass at Shinjuku Station West Exit. Omoide Yokocho (Memory Alley) is a narrow street filled with tiny, traditional restaurants and snack bars. Yakitori (grilled pieces of chicken) is the most common fare. This tightly packed alley, where little English is spoken, may not look like much but the food is great and local characters abound. It's a quintessential Tokyo experience. www.shinjuku-omoide.com/english/

Harajuku Fashion 原宿系ファッション   Harajuku is world famous for its street fashion – a new trend seems to appear every time you blink! Explore Takeshita Street through its clothing stores, snack shops and second hand finds. You'll be amazed by the creative fashion of the Tokyo youth who frequent this district. Continue on with a stroll down Omotesando, where the fashion will evolve from trendy youth to high-end designer retailers - housed in buildings that are just as impressive as the styles they hold.

Shibuya Crossing 渋谷スクランブル交差点   Departing Shibuya Station from the west side via the Hachiko Exit, you'll find yourself approaching the world's busiest pedestrian intersection, Shibuya Crossing. The streets that make up "The Scramble" lead to many fashionable shops and restaurants in this neighborhood. On the weekends, thousands will cross the intersection at one time – best to hold hands in the sea of people!

Ramen in Roppongi 六本木のラーメン   If you get hungry as you explore Tokyo, be sure to sample ramen, the well-known Japanese fast food. This delicious, slurp-able noodle soup can be found on almost any corner. One estimate states there are over 20,000 ramen shops throughout greater Tokyo. Ramen in Roppongi or Ginza – where will you eat?

Shimizuyu Onsen 温泉　清水湯   Shimizuyu Onsen offers a traditional Japanese spa-like experience that you would typically find in the mountains, but without having to leave Tokyo. Two different natural springs supply the bathing pools with essential minerals said to remedy physical ailments. Experiencing a traditional Japanese onsen is truly unique, just make sure to bathe before you soak!

Togoshi Tofu Shop 戸越銀座　豆腐屋   It may be more difficult to find these days, but to buy and eat tofu straight from the producer is sheer culinary joy. The Togoshi Ginza area has several individual shops that make a variety of delicacies from the simple soy bean. www.togoshiginza.jp/

Koinobori Streamers こいのぼり   Colorful koinobori (carp streamers) come out in great numbers in April and May to celebrate Children's Day. The city of Sagamihara in the Kanagawa prefecture of Tokyo raises over 2,000 koinobori, which appear to be swimming over the Sagami River during this national holiday.

Mount Fuji 富士山   Although Mount Fuji or "Fuji-san" is 100km (60 miles) from Tokyo, it can be seen on a clear day. Visiting this symbol of Japan is an easy day trip from Tokyo via the Shinkansen (high-speed train). Whether climbing, hiking or simply taking in its beauty up close, it's a breathtaking way to experience this World Heritage Site.

Kamakura – Great Buddha 鎌倉大仏   Another fantastic day trip from Tokyo is visiting The Great Buddha (Daibutsu) of Kamakura. Standing 11.3 meters tall (nearly four-stories high), this impressive statue was cast in bronze 750 years ago. While in Kamakura be sure to take in a few of the other shrines and temples this seaside town has to offer. www.kotoku-in.jp/en/top.html

Zojo-ji Temple & Tokyo Tower 増上寺と東京タワー   Zojo-ji Temple, built in 1393, houses the oldest wooden structure in Tokyo – the historic main gate Sangedatsuman. The gate's sections symbolize the three stages necessary to attain nirvana. Contrasting this ancient treasure and always in view, is the modern Tokyo Tower, an operational telecommunications tower built in 1958. Panoramic views of the city can be seen from its public observation deck.   www.zojoji.or.jp/en/   www.tokyotower.co.jp/eng/

Tea Ceremony 茶会   The tea ceremony is a refined ritual for the preparation and serving of a green tea called matcha. Filled with grace, eloquent movements, and tranquility, this ceremony embodies the Japanese aesthetic. Several hotels offer tea ceremony experiences, including our favorite spot to experience this beautiful art, Chosho-an in the Hotel Okura. www.hotelokura.co.jp/tokyo/en/special/chosho_an/

Fish Market 築地市場 (Tsukiji Market) and 豊洲市場 (Toyosu Market)   Every day, more than 400 varieties of fish and seafood are auctioned at Tokyo's fish markets. Tsukiji, the world's largest market, relocated its commercial operations less than 2 km away to modernized facilities at Toyosu in 2016. The auctions start bustling very early in the morning, while the adjacent market of small shops, restaurants, and fish vendors opens to the public later in the day.

Kabuki Theater 歌舞伎座   Kabuki is a traditional Japanese theater combining dance with drama featuring actors in elaborate traditional costumes and makeup. Most productions are three to four acts, but one act offerings are often available making an easier introduction for children or the uninitiated. The Kabuki-za in Ginza is the preeminent theater in Tokyo. www.kabuki-za.co.jp

COLORFUL TOKYO LOCATIONS

6 Imperial Palace 皇居 Situated in the heart of Tokyo, the Imperial Palace is the residence of Japan's Emperor and Empress. The large plaza surrounding the Palace offers a great view of the iconic bridges (Nijubashi) that lead to the inner grounds. Built on the former site of Edo Castle, the surrounding grounds include moats, massive stone walls and vast walkways, which are quite unique for this dense city. www.sankan.kunaicho.go.jp/

7 JR Train JR線 Trains are the most efficient way to get around Tokyo – whether it's the Japan Railways system or the Tokyo Metro. They're punctual, reasonably priced, with stops conveniently located throughout the city. Avoid the rush hours, if you can, where riders are pushed onto the trains by white-gloved attendants. Oh my! www.jreast.co.jp/e/

8 Taiyaki Vendor たい焼き屋 Taiyaki is a delicious fish-shaped, griddle-baked pastry filled with sweet azuki bean paste. Our favorite stop for this delicious delicacy is Yanagiya in the Ningyocho neighborhood. The shop started making taiyaki in 1916 and still uses fish molds that pre-date WWII. Be prepared to wait in line regardless of the day – but so worth it! www.ningyocho.or.jp/english/

9 Sumo Match 大相撲 Japanese wrestling, sumo, offers fast, dramatic action filled with ancient rituals that date back centuries. The great sumo hall of Tokyo, Ryogoku Kokugikan, hosts three of the six Japanese Grand Sumo Tournaments. With many wrestlers living in this area, a walk through the Ryogoku neighborhood results in frequent athlete sightings at restaurants or the train station. www.sumo.or.jp/en/

10 Akihabara - Vending Machines 秋葉原の自動販売機 Soup, umbrellas, coffee, and yes, even fresh fruit, can be found in vending machines in Akihabara and throughout Japan. This area of Tokyo is best known as the electronics district and offers an incomprehensible variety of electronic gadgets and computer gizmos. It's also a cultural hub for anime, manga and pop venues.

11 Senso-ji Temple 浅草寺 Guarded by Fujin (Wind God) and Raijin (Thunder God) at the front Kaminarimon (Thunder Gate), Senso-ji Temple in Asakusa is the oldest temple in Tokyo dating back to 645. The processional road to this Buddhist temple and surrounding area provide many traditional restaurants and unique shops. www.senso-ji.jp/about/index_e.html

12 Tokyo Skytree & Sumida River 東京スカイツリーと隅田川 Tradition meets modern. Just a short walk from Senso-ji is a fantastic view of Asakusa's modern architecture. Looking over the Sumida River is the Tokyo Skytree, a communications tower with observation deck and restaurants. Adjacent is the glass-of-beer shaped Asahi Beer Headquarters and the Flamme d'Or both designed by Philippe Starck. www.tokyo-skytree.jp/en/

13 Ueno Zoo 上野動物園 Ueno Zoo is home to 2,600 animals from 464 different species – from Sumatran tigers to giant pandas. Be sure to ride the raised monorail, to get a true bird's eye view of the diverse species living in their natural habitats. www.tokyo-zoo.net/english/ueno/

14 Ameyoko Market アメ横 From dried fish, to cowboy hats, to pineapple, you can find almost anything for sale in the 180 bustling shops of Ameyoko market. If you like bartering, crowded shopping stalls, and great prices, then this market is for you. Be prepared for a sensory explosion!

15 Kanda Festival 神田祭 The Kanda Festival (matsuri) based at Myojin Shrine is one of three great Shinto festivals in Tokyo. Many events take place over the festival weekend with a raucously fun street celebration for participants and observers alike. Musicians, characters dressed in traditional clothing and over 200 mikoshi (portable shrines) carried by large, festive teams help to celebrate wealth and good fortune. www.kandamyoujin.or.jp/

16 Ryokan Guest House 旅館 A ryokan is a Japanese guest house offering a taste of traditional culture, food and life. Guests sleep on futons with buckwheat pillows on tatami mat flooring. A traditional breakfast and dinner are typically included in the night's fee. One of our favorite guest houses is Homeikan, which is centrally located. A truly great way to immerse yourself in Japanese culture! www.homeikan.com

17 Nezu Shrine 根津神社 Nezu Shrine, one of Japan's oldest Shinto shrines, is set in beautifully serene grounds in central Tokyo. Over 50 varieties of azalea bushes deliver a colorful explosion in springtime. Tall cedars, gingko trees, and koi ponds provide a beautiful backdrop for the famous row of vermilion Torii gates that is said to take walkers from a secular place to a sacred one. www.nedujinja.or.jp/

18 Yanaka Ginza 谷中銀座 A ginza is a bustling street that offers many selections for daily shopping - fruit and vegetables, tofu, fish, tea, and household supplies each typically sold at separate stores. With only a few areas like this left in Tokyo, the traditional neighborhood of Yanaka is worth exploring. Look for the beckoning cat (maneko-neko) at many shops, which is a good luck charm to bring in customers.

29 Hanami at Asukayama Park 飛鳥山公園の花見 Hanami, or enjoying cherry blossoms (sakura), is a treasured rite of springtime at many parks in Japan. Asukayama Park is a quintessential spot to bring a picnic and a few friends to take in this beautiful season.

30 Kendo Dojo 剣道道場 Kendo, or the "Way of the Sword," is a traditional martial art descended from samurai warriors. Today, however, a bamboo sword is used instead of steel. Participants wear body armor for protection in matches, which are held in a practice area or "dojo". Dojos are found all over Tokyo, but we're most familiar with Tokyo Kyumeikan Kendo Dojo where classes can be found in English. www.bekkoame.ne.jp/~kyumeikan/homenglish.htm

HARAJIIKU FASHION

SHIBUYA CROSSING

RAMEN IN ROPPONGI

SHIMIZUYU ONSEN

KOINOBORI STREAMERS

MOUNT FUJI

KAMAKURA - GREAT BUDDHA

ZOJO-JI TEMPLE & TOKYO TOWER

FISH MARKET

KABUKI THEATER

IMPERIAL PALACE

TAIYAKI VENDOR

SUMO MATCH

SENSO-JI TEMPLE

TOKYO SKYTREE & SUMIDA RIVER

UENO ZOO

AMEYOKO MARKET

RYOKAN GUEST HOUSE

NEZU SHRINE

HANAMI AT ASUKAYAMA PARK

KENDO DOJO

DRAW A COLORFUL PLACE IN THE WORLD YOU WOULD LIKE TO EXPLORE

For more books in this series visit us at: www.colorfulcities.com

100% designed, illustrated and printed in the USA.

Concept, design & text: Laura Lahm
Illustrations: Steph Calvert
Covers coloring: Julie Knutson

ISBN: 978-0-9898972-1-1

"Domo Arigato Gozaimasu" (thank you very much!) to my amazing reviewers, editors and Tokyo explorers: Kirk, Astrid, Seth, Maria, Akiko, Junko, Mami, Jenna, NBO! and Nakao-san.

For my father, Roger – Thanks for kindling my initial spark to explore
Colorful Tokyo! Love, LL

For my sister, Michelle – Your happy place is calling.
Go Banana! Love, Steph